TRINITY
COLLEGE LONDON PRESS

G R A D E **05**

SINGING

Songs & Teaching Notes for
Trinity College London
Exams 2018–2021

Includes CD of
piano accompaniments
and pronunciation guides

Published by
Trinity College London Press
trinitycollege.com

Registered in England
Company no. 09726123

Printed in England by Caligraving Ltd.

My Lagan Love

Seosamh MacCathmaoil

Trad.
arr. Harty
(1879-1941)

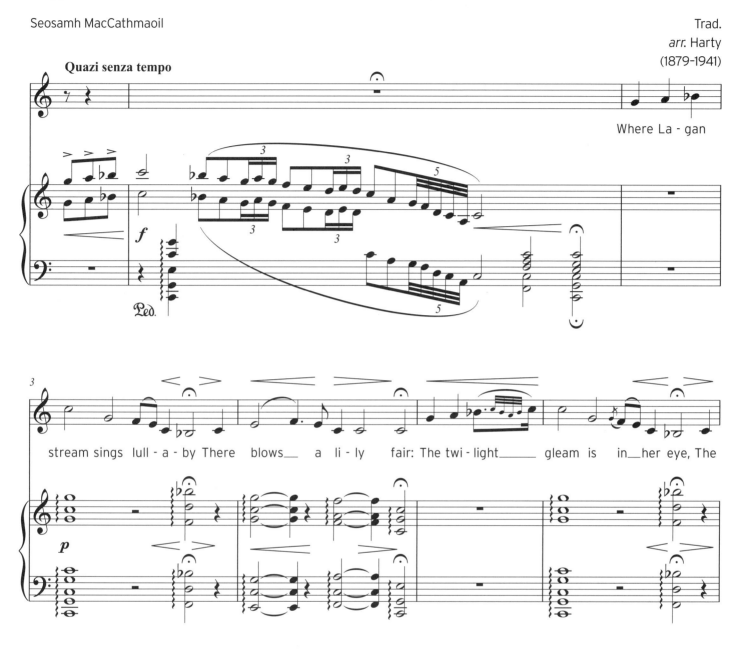

Quazi senza tempo

Where La - gan

stream sings lull - a - by There blows___ a li - ly fair: The twi - light____ gleam is in__her eye, The

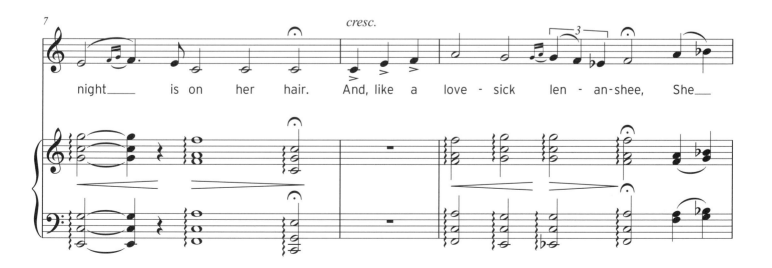

night____ is on her hair. And, like a love - sick len - an - shee, She___

hath my heart__ in thrall; Nor life I owe, nor li-ber-ty, For Love__ is lord of all.

And oft-en when the beet-le's horn Hath

lull - ed the eve to sleep, I steal un - to her shiel-ing lorn, And

through__ the door - ing peep. There on the crick - et's sing - ing-stone She__

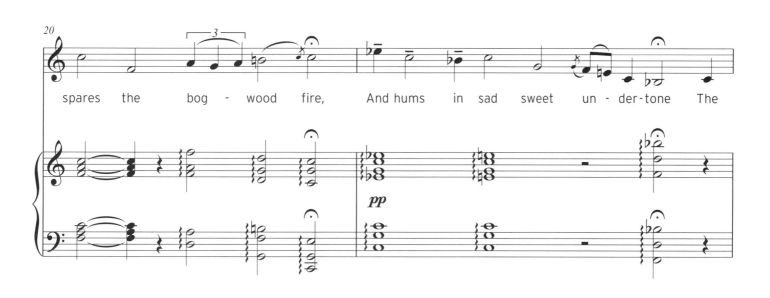

spares the bog - wood fire, And hums in sad sweet un - der-tone The

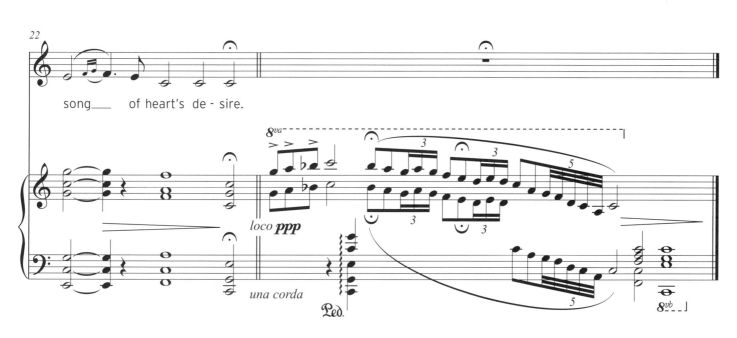

song__ of heart's de - sire.

Fair, if You Expect Admiring

Words and music by
Thomas Campion
(1567–1620)

love's de - light - - ing. Then when hope is lost and___
long la - ment - - ing. But if griefs re - main still___

love is scorn - ed I'll bu - ry my de-sires and quench the fires That
un - re - dress - ed I'll fly to her a - gain and sue for pi - ty

ev - er yet in vain have burn - ed. I'll bu - ry my de-sires and
to re - new my hopes dis - tress - ed. I'll fly to her a - gain and

quench the fires That ev - er yet in vain have burn - ed.
sue for pi - ty to re - new my hopes dis - tress - ed.

Vieni, vieni o mio diletto

Come, come, oh my beloved, that my all-loving heart waits for you and calls every hour.
My all-loving heart waits for you and calls every hour.

Antonio Salvi
(1664–1724)

Antonio Vivaldi
(1678–1741)
arr. Holloway

Include all repeats in the exam.

Il mio cor'e tutto a-ffe - tto, Il mio co - r'e tu-tto affe - tto

gia____ t'a - spe - tta e gia__ ti__ chia____ ma,__ ti

chia - ma. chia - ma.

Oiseau, si tous les ans

Ariette, K. 307 (284d)

Birds, you change climate every year as soon as the sad winter strips our groves;
not only for a change of foliage or to avoid the foggy winter weather,
but your destiny does not allow you to love beyond the season of flowers.
When springtime is gone, you look for another place to sustain love all year round.

Antoine Ferrand
(1678-1719)

Wolfgang Amadeus Mozart
(1756-1791)

Oi - seaux, si tous les ans vous chan - gez de cli - mats, vous chan - gez de cli - mats, dès que le tris - te hi - ver dé - pouil - le nos bo - ca - ges; ce n'est pas seu - le - ment pour

chan-ger de_ feuil - la - ges, ni pour é - vi - ter nos_ fri-

-mats; mais vo - tre dé - sti - née, mais vo - tre dé - sti - née ne

vous_____ per - met, ne vous per - met_ d'ai - mer, qu'à

la sai - son des fleurs. Et quand el - le pas -

11

Der Blumenstrauss

(The Nosegay)

She strolls in the flower garden, surveying the colourful scene, while all the little flowers are waiting, looking up to her.
'You, heralds of springtime, bearing the latest news, bring my message to the one who loves me truly.'
She makes a selection of flowers and prepares a beautiful bouquet, shyly offering it to her friend while avoiding his gaze.
But there is no need to ask what the flowers and colours mean, when the sweetest spring is conveyed through her eyes.

Karl Klingemann
(1798-1862)

Felix Mendelssohn
(1809-1847)

Sie wan - delt im Blu - men - gar - ten und mu - stert den bun - ten Flor,_____ und al - le die Klei - nen war - ten und schau-en zu ihr em - por. "Und

13

seid ihr denn Früh - lings - bo - - - ten, ver -

-kün - dend was stets___ so neu,_____ so___ wer-det auch mei - ne

Bo - ten an ihn, der mich liebt so treu, an

ihn,_____ der___ mich liebt_____ so___

treu."

cresc.   *sf*   *sf*   dim.

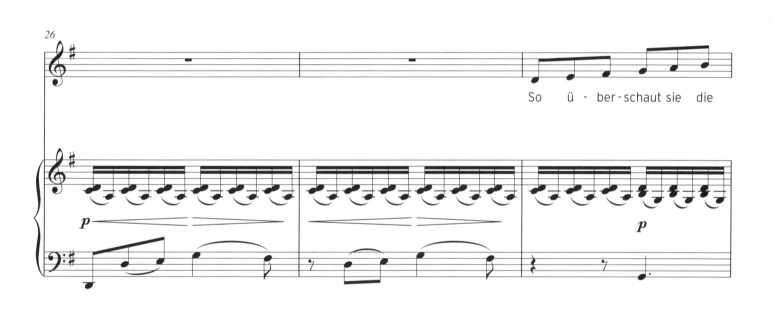

So ü - ber - schaut sie die

p   *p*

Ha - be und ord - net den lieb - li - chen Strauss,_____ und

reicht_ dem Freun-de die Ga - be, und weicht sei-nem Bli - cke aus. Was

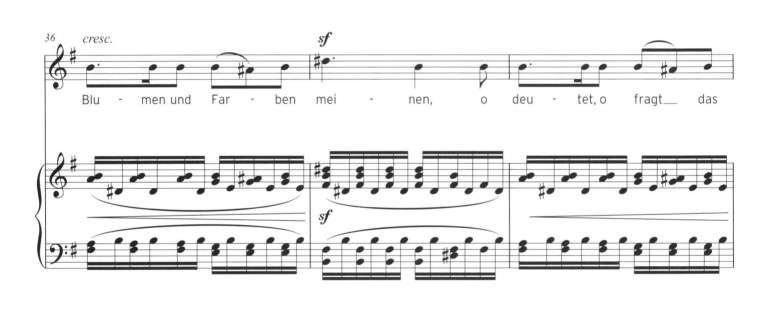

Blu - men und Far - ben mei - nen, o deu - tet, o fragt_ das

nicht,_____ wenn aus den Au-gen der Ei - nen der sü - sse-ste Früh - ling

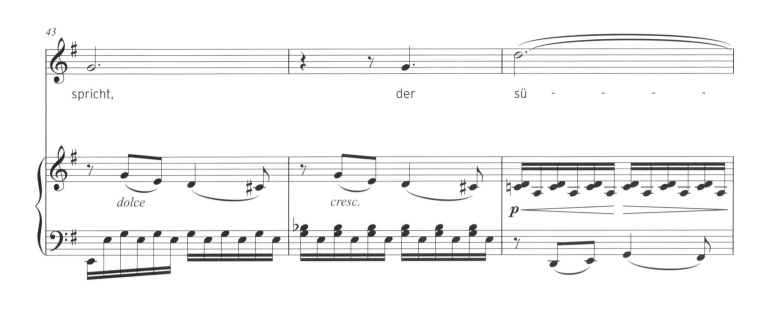

spricht, der sü - - - -

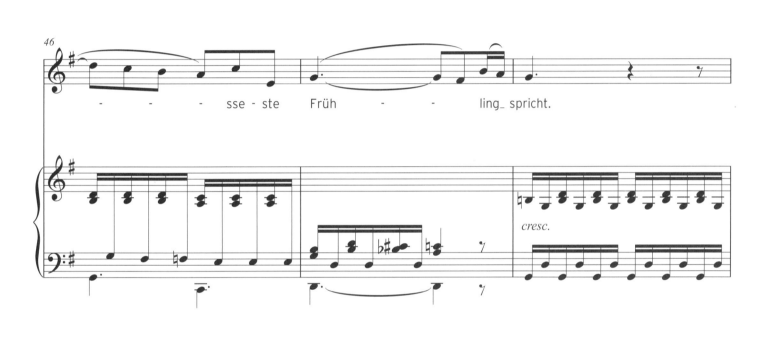

- - - sse - ste Früh - - ling_ spricht.

Waldeinsamkeit

op. 76 no. 3

(The Quiet of the Woods)

Yesterday evening, all was still. I watched a blackbird, as I sat there quietly reflecting.
My sweetheart caught me unaware, softly creeping up and kissing me.

Max Reger
(1873–1916)

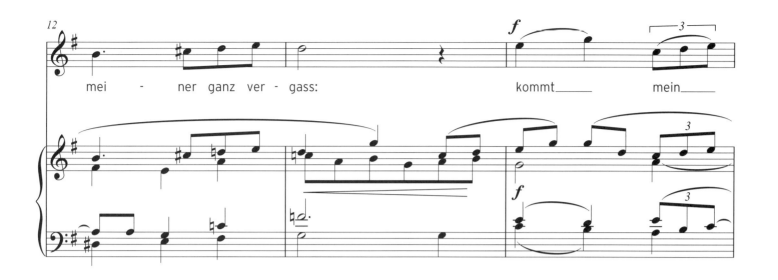

mei - ner ganz ver - gass: kommt_____ mein_____

Schatz_____ und schlei - chet sich um mich_____ und

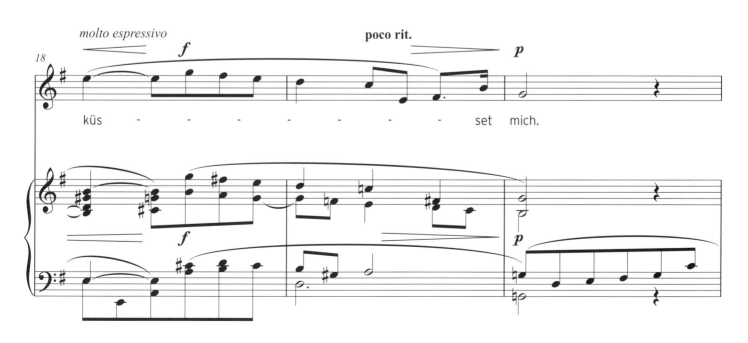

küs - - - - - - - set mich.

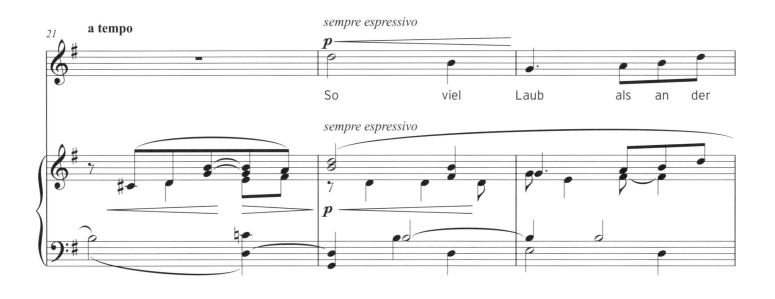

So viel Laub als an der

Lin - den ist und so viel tau - send -

- mal hat mich mein Schatz___ ge - küsst; denn ich muss ge -

-steh'n,   denn ich muss ge - steh'n, es hat's

nie - mand ge - seh'n, und die Am - sel soll mein Zeu - ge sein:

molto espressivo   **rit.**

wir_____ war'n al - lein.

By the Sea

from *Four Songs of the Sea*, op. 1

Words and music by
Roger Quilter
(1877–1953)

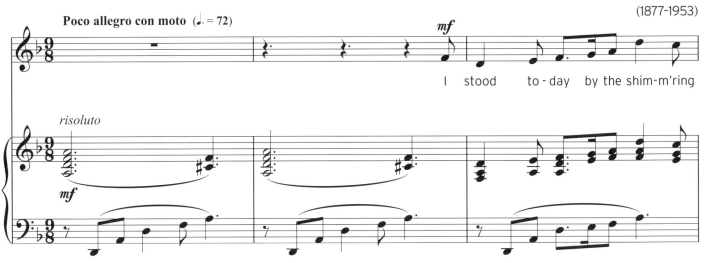

I stood to-day by the shim-m'ring

sea;_____ Nev - er was wind_____ so mild__ and free;_____ The

light and the love - li - ness daz - zled me,_____

Cantique

To all lost, crying souls, I open within the stars my hands full of prayers.
All sin will be absolved when love has spoken. No soul can die when love has cried
and if love is lost on the trails of this world, tears will guide me along the way.

Maurice Maeterlinck

Nadia Boulanger
(1887-1979)

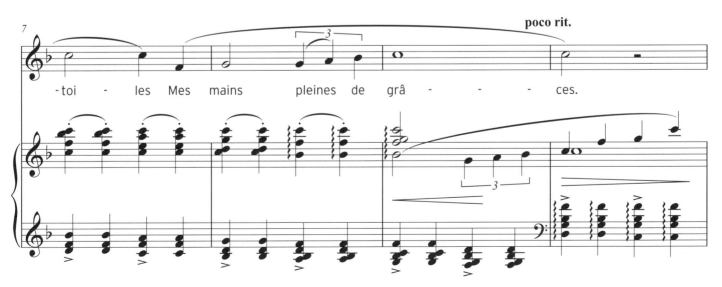

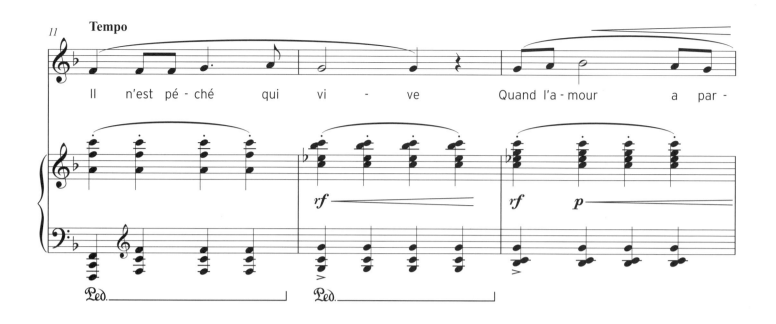

Il n'est pé - ché qui vi - ve Quand l'a - mour a par -

- lé Il n'est â - me qui meu - re Quand l'a -

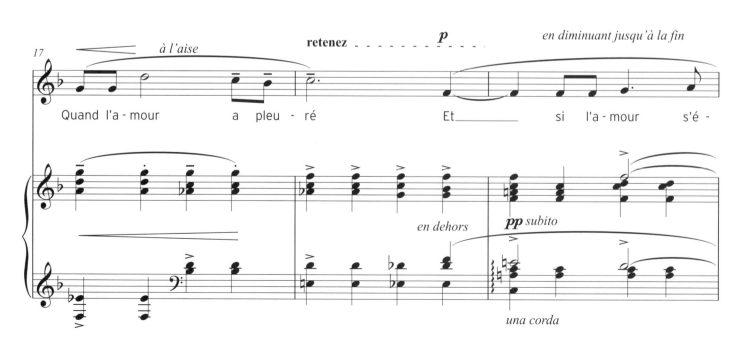

Quand l'a - mour a pleu - ré Et____ si l'a - mour s'é -

-ga - re   Aux sen - tiers d'i - ci - bas   Ses

lar - mes   me re - trou - vent   Et   ne s'é - ga - rent

ppp mais bien soutenu

suivez

pas.

for Jan

Come Live with Me and Be My Love

Christopher Marlowe
(1564–1593)

Alan Bullard
(b. 1947)

Come live with me and be___ my love, And

we___ will all the plea - sures prove That hills___ and val - leys, dales and

fields, And all___ the crag - gy moun - tain yields.___

kir - tle Em-broi - der'd all___ with leaves_ of myr - tle;

A gown_ made of the fin - est wool Which from___ our pret-ty

lambs_ we pull; Fair___ lined slip-pers for___ the cold, With buck - les

of___ the pur - est gold;___ A

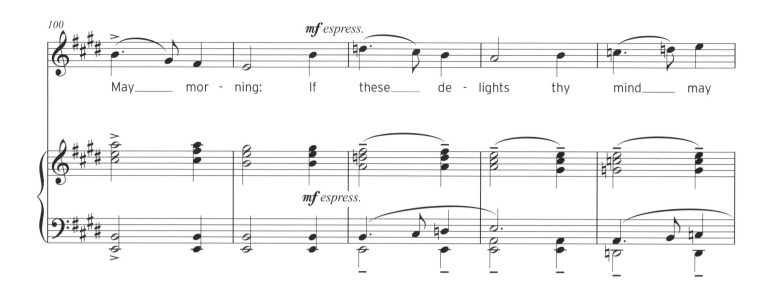

May____ mor - ning: If these____ de - lights thy mind____ may

move, Then live_____ with me and____ be my

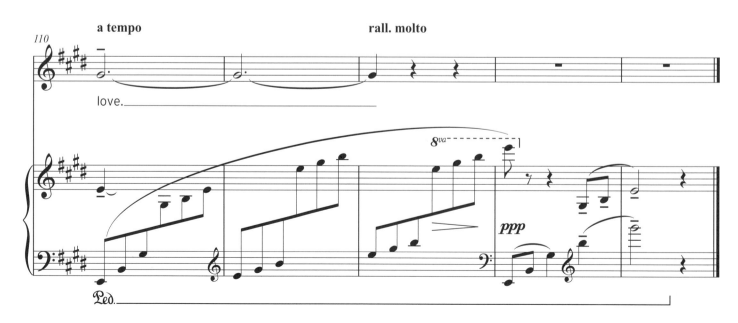

love._____

Ped._____

The Phoenix

Bez Berry

Jeffery Wilson
(b. 1957)

My eyes of spark-ling sapph-ires glow

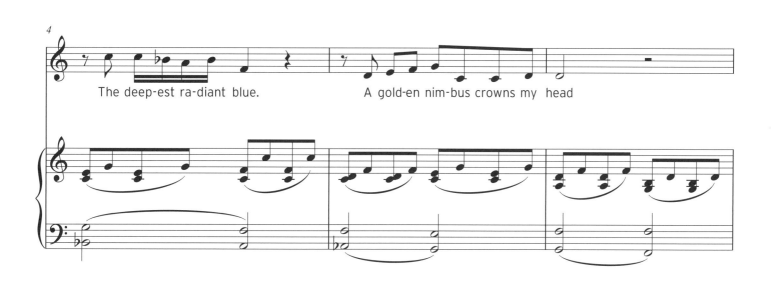

The deep-est ra-diant blue. A gold-en nim-bus crowns my head

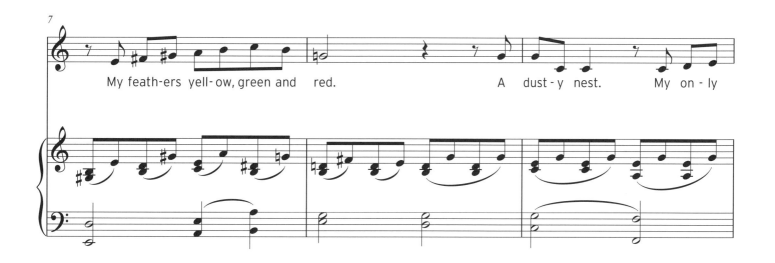

My feath-ers yell-ow, green and red. A dust-y nest. My on-ly

33

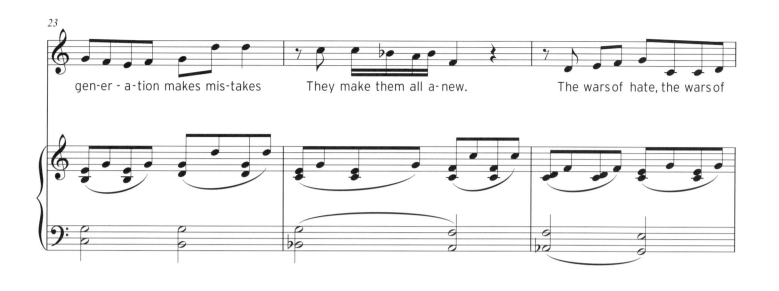

gen-er - a-tion makes mis-takes | They make them all a-new. | The wars of hate, the wars of

greed, | The hate of race, of co-lour, creed. | There is no point, there is no

need. | Oh what's a bird to do? | And so I will be born a-

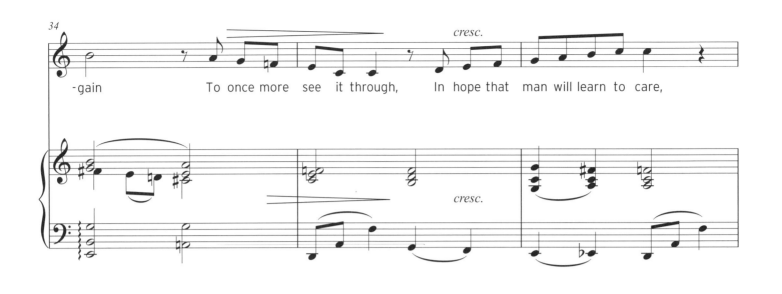

-gain　　　　　To once more see it through,　　In hope that man will learn to care,

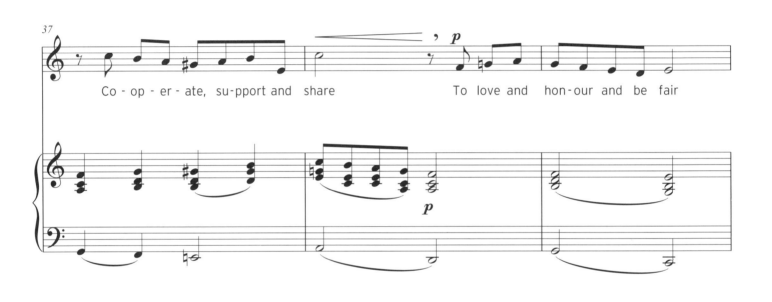

Co - op - er - ate, su-pport and share　　　To love and hon-our and be fair

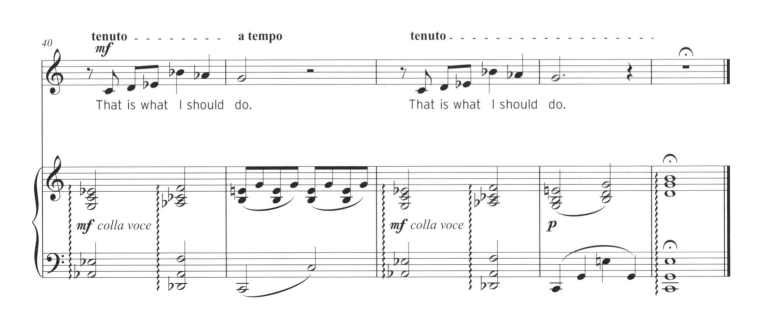

That is what I should do.　　　　That is what I should do.

Fear No More the Heat o' the Sun

from *Cymbeline* Act 4, Scene 2

William Shakespeare
(1564–1616)

Ian Higginson
(b. 1959)

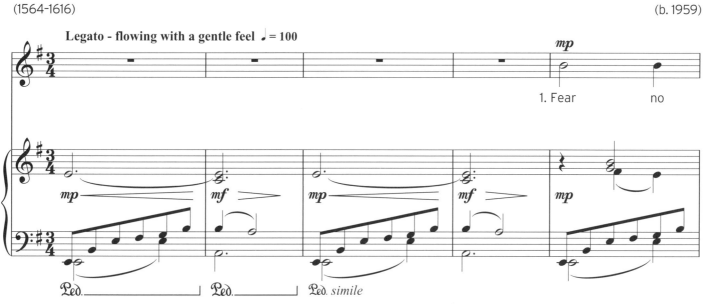

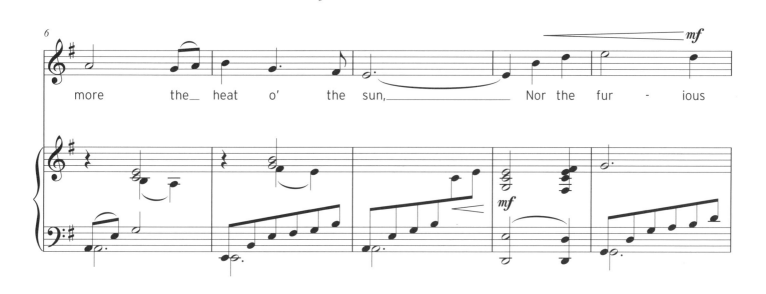

must_____ All foll - ow this,___ and come__ to

dust._____ 3. Fear no more the_

light - ning flash_____ Nor the all - - dread - ed

thun - der - stone; Fear not slan - der,__

cen - sure rash;_____ Thou hast fin - ish'd joy_ and

moan:_____ All lov-ers young, all lov - ers

must_____ Con - sign to thee,_ and come_ to dust._____

Lullaby

Dorothy Parker

Robert James Stove
(b. 1961)

Sleep, pret - ty la - dy, the night is en -

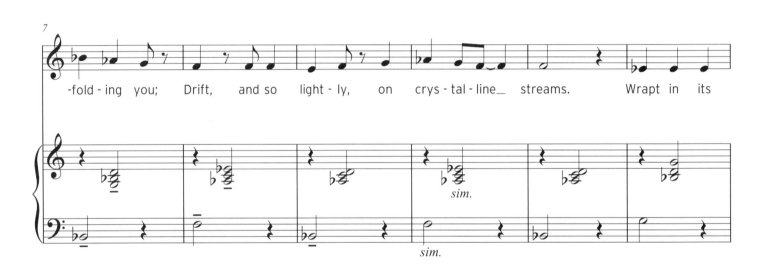

-fold - ing you; Drift, and so light - ly, on crys - tal - line_ streams. Wrapt in its

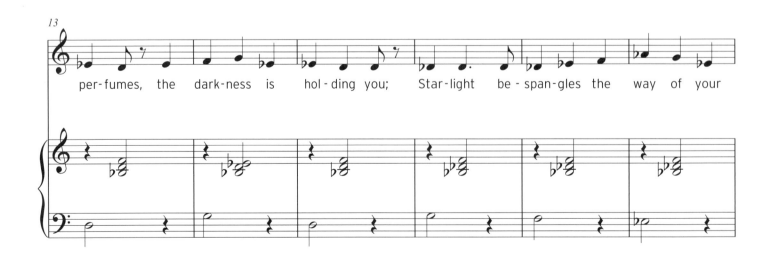

per - fumes, the dark - ness is hol - ding you; Star - light be - span - gles the way of your

dreams. Cho - rus the night - in - gales wist - ful - ly am - or - ous; Bles - sed - ly

qui - et, the blare of the day; All the sweet hours may your vi - sions be

rall. a tempo

glam - or - ous; Sleep, pret - ty la - dy, as long as you may. Sleep pret - ty

la - dy, the night shall be still for you; Sil - ver'd and si - lent, it wat - ches you

rest. Each lit - tle____ breeze in its eag - er - ness will for you Mur - mur the

me - lo - dies____ an - cient and blest. So in the mid - night does hap - pi - ness____

cap - ture us; Morn - ing is dim with a - noth - er day's tears,____

Give your - self sweet - ly to im - a - ges____ rap - tur - ous; Sleep, pret - ty

Teaching notes

Trad. *arr.* Harty   My Lagan Love   page 3

'My Lagan Love' is a traditional Irish air from Northern Donegal with English words by Seosamh MacCathmaoil (Joseph Campbell). It seems likely that the Lagan of the title refers to the river that eventually runs into Belfast. There is a reference to a character from Irish mythology in the poem: a 'lenanshee' or 'lennan sidhe' in Gaelic is a type of Irish fairy who would take the love of mortals and then abandon them. The 'shieling lorn' in the second verse is a 'little shack' and the cricket is an insect traditionally associated with good luck. The meaning of the 'beetle's horn' is slightly unclear though it is possible that it is the strumming sound that some beetles can make.

This song was most probably traditionally sung *a cappella* but in this version the Irish composer and conductor, Hamilton Harty has arranged it with a piano accompaniment. There is no time signature given as the instruction *quasi senza tempo* suggests that the song is to be sung with freedom and rhythmic flexibility just as it would have been when sung unaccompanied. However, you have to make it fit with the piano so try practising singing with a strong and consistent underlying pulse, keeping all of the rhythms exactly as notated. This will help you to get a feel for the movement of the song and also establish a good connection with your accompaniment. Use the pauses at the end of each line judiciously, not making them so long that the whole keeps coming to a complete halt. As you start to feel the way one line flows into the next you can loosen the pulse a little but ensure that the whole song still retains an overall sense of cohesion. There are a few embellishments or ornaments added at times to the melody and this is in keeping with the song's Irish folk origins. Practise the song without the additions at first and then put them in very neatly and quickly so that they do not interrupt the overall sweep of the melodic lines.

See if you can find some contrasting interpretations of this song and listen to how different singers convey its character.

Campion   Fair, if You Expect Admiring   page 6

Thomas Campion was an English composer, poet and medic. He composed music for the popular entertainments of the day called Masques and along with composers such as Rosseter and Dowland helped to develop the English lute song, producing over one hundred of his own compositions.

The text of this song first asks the fair one to reciprocate the lover's affection. However, the lover says that if the fair one is untrue then she should flee from love and, if that is the case, he will accept that his love is scorned and extinguish his passion. In the second verse the lover asks the fates and the stars to take pity on him and begs time to be the healer of his pain. However, if despite his pleas, his grief at being rejected still remains, he will return to the fair one once again to beg for her pity and see if she will relent and return his love.

Campion is said to have favoured 'straightforward delivery' of his songs and so this song needs to be sung with clear bright tone and neat precision. Some of the words sound strange to modern ears so keep them all distinct, remembering that words like 'scorned' and 'burned' are divided into two syllables. The running passages should be sung with care, keeping the voice very agile and ensuring that the descending ones do not go flat or the ascending ones sharp. You will need to enunciate the words with especial care and lightness of touch in these passages. Try saying them out loud in precise rhythm, feeling how much you need to articulate the consonants. Make sure that repeated notes are all pitched accurately with no drift in tuning between them and be quick on the pick up after the $\frac{2}{4}$ bars. As Campion himself did not give a definitive tempo marking for the song, you could practise this at different speeds until you find one that you feel captures the essence of the song and allows you to sing with easy control.

The lute was a very popular instrument for accompanying songs in the late 16th century. What can you find out about the lute? Try to find recordings of musicians playing the lute to give you an idea of the sort of sound it makes. Do you think that it would be very different singing this song being accompanied by a lute rather than the piano?

Vivaldi   Vieni, vieni o mio diletto   page 8

Antonio Vivaldi was a highly prolific musician, teacher and composer who also studied for the Priesthood. His many compositions include over 500 concertos and 46 operas. This aria comes from the opera *Ercole su'l Termodonte* and though the full score of this opera is lost, many of the arias, including this one, have survived in manuscript form.

Baroque operatic arias often had set forms and 'Vieni, Vieni' is one of those being in an AABB structure. It is important that each section is repeated in performance as this gives the singer the opportunity to add some ornaments or embellishments the second time through. This practice was very common in baroque music as it was felt that the additions helped enhance the emotional expression within the music. It also made listening to a repeated melody more interesting for the audience.

A common ornament was the trill or shake and these would usually be found at cadence points in a piece. Cadences come at the end of a phrase or section of a piece of music so they are rather like punctuation. Where a text would use commas or full stops for example, music would use different cadences. Both sections of this aria end with perfect cadences and these provide an opportunity for you to try adding a trill. A trill is simply a rapid alternation between the note written in the music and the note above it. A good exercise to practise is singing two notes that sit either a tone or a semitone apart in even rhythm, first very slowly then gradually getting faster and faster. Don't worry if you find this hard. Just have some fun trying!

Do you know any other compositions by Vivaldi? See if you can find some recordings of other vocal or instrumental music that he wrote to listen to. Can you spot any ornaments being added?

Mozart   Oiseau, si tous les ans   page 10

Mozart was an Austrian born musician and composer who began writing music from a very early age. He has over 600 compositions to his name in all genres but he particularly loved the sound of the human voice and composed many vocal works including operas, cantatas, Masses, concert arias and songs. He used texts in different languages but only wrote two of his songs in French.

Although this song was written when he was still in his early twenties, it shows the influence of the opera, being composed in the style of an *arietta*, like those usually found in French *opéra comique*. It is almost a mini-drama, with the piano and the voice both expressing the meaning of the words with musical effects. The opening with its short, dotted phrases could suggest the hopping of the birds and you need to sing with a really crisp delineation of the rhythm. As the piano part changes to begin to imitate the birds' wings with all the delicate grace notes that 'flutter' across the arpeggios, you need to ensure that the triplets are sung very smoothly and evenly. Give the pause on the high note plenty of time before you move into the minor section where the piano takes over the moving triplets. After this, short precise phrases return for both singer and pianist and you need to be absolutely together. The piano imitates the twittering of the birds with its repeated high note before a return to the dotted patterns for the singer, bringing the song to a joyful, spirited close. Plan your breathing in this last section as you only have time for a very quick breath, which should go with the meaning of the words and come after 'l'année'.

As this is a song full of character, work out how you will use your eyes and face to help convey the meaning to your listeners. There is an almost 'cheeky' feel to parts of the song and you may be tempted to add in some gestures but, if you do, be careful not to over-use them or they will simply become a distraction.

Mendelssohn — Der Blumenstrauss — page 13

Felix Mendelssohn was a German musician of the early Romantic period. He was a child prodigy displaying exceptional ability as a child and writing his first symphony when he was only 15. Perhaps more famous for his orchestral writing, he nevertheless composed many solo songs and duets though unlike some of his contemporaries, he favoured relatively simply piano accompaniments that would not detract from the words of the songs.

This song is a 'strophic' song, where the music for the two verses is the same. The almost continuous motion in the piano part means that you have to sing your lines very accurately to fit yet continue to think of how each note flows into the next, creating a smooth *legato*. The opening melodic lines are all rising phrases, stepping up successively in pitch. You need to feel how these gradually build, drawing the music forward. You could try singing them just on one vowel at first to feel the natural shape of the music before adding in the words. The final phrase of each verse is long so think about planning your breathing. You should aim to sing them each in one breath if possible, practising more quickly at first to gain confidence in singing them through before slowing the speed down. Make sure that you sustain the first long held note of each with plenty of breath but remember not to use all your air just on this one note.

Is it easier to sing a song where all the verses have the same music or where the music is different? Do you think that the singer has to work harder to communicate effectively in a 'strophic' song?

Reger — Waldeinsamkeit — page 18

Max Reger was a German composer, pianist, organist, conductor and teacher. He wrote over 300 songs but many are not well known today. They are often complicated with demanding writing for both singer and accompanist but this song has a very memorable line and an accessible piano part.

There is a lovely delicacy and beauty in the song, which needs to be brought out by using all the composer's dynamic markings to create a performance full of expression. There are some climactic f moments but overall the mood is tender and peaceful as the two lovers alone together in the calm of the evening enjoy their 'kisses'.

The doubling of the vocal line in the piano enhances the way the phrases rise and fall and you need to keep your singing very smooth. So take care that you manage to keep a true sense of *legato* whilst at the same time ensuring that the words are still enunciated. Try keeping the vowel sounds really open and long, ensuring that you never close into the consonants at the ends of words too quickly. You could try practising this song just singing the vowels of the words with no consonants added. This will help you to feel how each one flows into the next. Don't overwork the jaw too much but instead feel how the shape inside the mouth changes as the tongue moves.

The two verses of this song are virtually identical but what do you notice about the phrases that come at the end of each verse? There are two subtle differences, one of tempo and one of rhythm so think how you can draw these out in your performance.

Quilter — By the Sea — page 22

Roger Quilter was an English composer though he studied at the Hoch Conservatory in Frankfurt, Germany. He is particularly known for his songs, writing well over one hundred in his lifetime.

This song is one of his very early songs, being part of a set of *Songs of the Sea* that received their first performance in 1900. The setting is of Quilter's own words and he uses both the voice and the piano to suggest rising and falling of the waves. A dotted rhythmic pattern passes between the singer and the accompaniment expressing the energy of the tide, though in the middle verse, the vocal line becomes smoother and broader as the singer contemplates the mystery of the sea while the piano continues to surge from low notes to high. In order to match the sonority of the accompaniment, you need to produce a rich and ringing tone. Make sure that you don't force the sound through the throat though as you need to keep the throat muscles relaxed as you sing. You could try some gentle head rolls before you start your practice to loosen off any tension and then try humming at different pitches in your range. This gentle exercise will also ensure that you have plenty of forward resonance in the voice, which will help with projection, especially as you move to the fuller sounds of the f passages in the song.

The sea has inspired many poets and musicians. If you have the chance to spend time by the sea, could you write your own poem about how the sea makes you feel? Can you also find other songs about the sea that you could listen to and learn?

Boulanger — Cantique — page 25

Nadia Boulanger was a French composer, teacher and conductor. At the age of 10 she became a student at the Paris Conservatoire, studying with Widor and Fauré among others. After the death of her father when she was 13, she worked as a pianist and teacher but aimed to win the prestigious Prix de Rome for composition. She did not achieve this ambition, instead going on to a substantial career in conducting, becoming the first woman to conduct many orchestras in America and Europe. She also continued teaching and influenced many composers including Aaron Copland and Philip Glass.

A *cantique* is a hymn and although the words are from a Catholic poem, their message is more universally spiritual with the message that love will always triumph.

The song demands a beautifully sustained line with notes held evenly on controlled breath pressures. You need to ensure that your posture is good, with excellent muscular balance, to allow the breath to flow without unwanted constriction. Much of the singing in the final part is very soft. Don't allow the energy to drop as you sing quietly but aim to keep fullness and focus of tone, with a projected sound not holding back by constricting the throat or tightening the jaw. Practise some longer held notes with a comfortable mf sound before singing them more quietly, concentrating on not allowing the sound to become breathy or too held back.

There are many performance directions in French in this song, both for the singer and the pianist. Make sure that you find out what each one means before you sing so that you can stay true to the composer's intentions in your performance.

Alan Bullard studied with Herbert Howells at the Royal College of Music in London and went on to become the Head of Composition at the Colchester Institute. He is now a full-time composer writing in most genres for both amateur and professional musicians.

The words to 'Come Live with Me and Be My Love' are by Christopher Marlowe, a poet and playwright, who was a direct contemporary of Shakespeare. Also known as 'The Passionate Shepherd to His Love', it is a joyful love poem set in an idealised vision of the countryside. The poem has a regular metre and rhythm and Bullard enhances this repeated pattern of movement in his setting with the $\frac{3}{4}$ time signature almost having a feeling of one in a bar with the *allegro con brio* pace of the song. He also uses a recurrent dotted rhythmic motif, which adds an injection of energy and impetus to phrases. So make sure in your singing that you feel the forward pull of each of the lines, supplying each one with a warm, full tone ably sustained by firm breath pressure. Inhalation will often need to be quick so keep the abdomen muscles working efficiently, ensuring that you are not drawing air in with too much work from the upper body. Phrases too move quickly across the lower and middle registers of the voice so you need to keep the tone colour consistent from the lowest to highest notes.

The composer has added many changes of dynamics and tempo in this song so think how you can use each one to enhance your communication of the changing pastoral scenes. How do you think that the various changes of key help to enrich expression?

Wilson   The Phoenix   page 33

Jeffery Wilson is a composer and jazz musician. He studied at the Royal College of Music in London and his performances and recordings range from popular and jazz to classical and contemporary. In addition, he works as a teacher, adjudicator and examiner.

The text of this song is all about the mythical bird called the Phoenix. Legend has it that the Phoenix is a magical bird of radiant beauty that can live for up to one thousand years before it dies by bursting into flames. It is then reborn from the ashes and starts its life all over again. Not only closely connected with fire it is also associated with the sun and so has brilliantly coloured feathers along with sparkling sapphire blue eyes. It is often seen in paintings with a nimbus, or luminous halo like cloud, surrounding its head suggesting its supernatural qualities.

The whole song is based on a repeated question: 'Oh what's a bird to do?' which is set to a very distinctive 'tag' or repeated musical idea, which needs to be sung with very careful tuning whilst observing the *tenuto* instruction. The direction to the pianist *colla voce* means 'with the voice' so your accompanist will wait for you on the rolled chords. The exact same 'tag' appears at the very end of the song, this time with the answer: 'That is what I should do'. Make sure you enunciate these very clearly, thinking about how you might vary the *tenuto* the second time to add even more emphasis to the resolution.

All of the musical phrases throughout the song are short so you need to make sure that you connect them mentally and always feel that one moves into the next even with rests in between so that the whole does not become too fragmented.

Are there any other characters you have read about or seen in films that are able to regenerate or be reborn? And what do you think might be the advantages or disadvantages of being able to live for a very long time?

Ian Higginson studied conducting under Sir David Willcocks but also works as an organist, accompanist and teacher as well as a composer.

The words to this song are by Shakespeare and come from one of his later plays called *Cymbeline*. The plot of the play is particularly complicated but at this point in the play in Act 4 Scene 2, two of the characters are mourning the apparent death of their friend. So the mood of this song is elegiac as the words unfold with the theme that death comes to everyone from wealthy 'golden lads' to impoverished 'chimney sweepers'. Even rulers, teachers and doctors as symbolised by 'the sceptre, learning and physic' come to the dust of death. Whilst death means that someone can no longer experience the joys of life, it is seen as a positive thing too as it liberates a person from the worries of how to find food and clothes to wear and from the tyranny of others.

The three verses of the song are all very similar but you can use vocal 'effects' to 'paint' the different pictures. Think for example how you might use a slight stress on the first 'f' of furious or on the 'fr' of frown. The composer has written an accent over the first syllable of 'lightning' so really use the tongue to give a good flick on the 'l' sound. You could also emphasise the 'sh' sound on the word 'flash'. At the very end of the song you have a long held note so it might be an idea to breathe before the word 'to' in order to make sure you have sufficient air to finish the song well.

Higginson has only set three of the four verses of Shakespeare's poem as it appears in *Cymbeline*. A number of other composers have set these words from Shakespeare's *Cymbeline* either for solo voice or voices or for choirs. These include Finzi, Quilter, Sondheim, Ronald Corp and Vaughan Williams (his setting is called *Dirge for Fidele*). Try listening to some of these different versions and see which ones you think are the most effective.

Stove   Lullaby   page 42

R J Stove is an Australian composer, editor, broadcaster and writer whose books include biographies of the composers Palestrina and Franck as well as a *Student's Guide to Musical History*.

In this song he has set words by the American poet, Dorothy Parker who was writing in the first half of the 20th century. She was well known for her wit and the comic twists she put in her poems and this lullaby is no exception. Usually, a lullaby is sung by an adult to a child but this one is different for here it is more of a love song. The first part details the beauties of the night with its starlight and breezes and 'crystalline streams'. The poem goes on to suggest that day is not so happy and peaceful and so the narrator wishes the lady to sleep for 'a couple of years'. The real point of the poem though only comes at the end when we realise that the singer is actually in love with the sleeper and is hoping that she will stay asleep because her beauty is so great that when she is awake everyone falls in love with her. While she is asleep though the narrator might have a chance at love.

The composer uses two alternating sections of music that are very similar to each other in this song. This helps to highlight the contrasts in the words between night and day but also gives an almost hypnotic feel to the waltzing motion of the $\frac{3}{4}$ metre, readily suggesting the mood of a lullaby. Once you have learnt the song you will not find the shifts of key particularly difficult to negotiate, though do take especial care as you slow down for the final section where the piano moves from chords to more intricate arpeggiated passages.

The rhythms do need attention as slight shifts occur throughout with some hints of syncopation at times. Think very carefully about how you will shape the ending of this song, as your listeners really need to pick up on the 'twist'.

Are there other songs or pieces of music that you know that contain a surprise? This could be in the words or even in the music itself.